The View from Under the Pew

Diane Winters Johnson
Illustrations by Margaret Freed

Abingdon Press
Nashville

Dedicated to the men and women of The Seeing Eye for their tireless energy, love, and work in the care and training of dogs like Walter who guide the blind through their lives in work and ministry. "The hearing ear and the seeing eye—the LORD has made them both." (Proverbs 20:12, NRSV)

Diane Winters Johnson

For my parents, Richard and Margaret. Thank you for the years of support and encouragement.

Margaret Freed

The View from Under the Pew

Text copyright © 2004 by Rev. Diane Winters Johnson.
Illustrations copyright © 2005 by Margaret Freed.
All rights reserved.

First Edition
Published 2008 by Abingdon Press

The Seeing Eye Inc. is a registered trademark. Only dogs trained at The Seeing Eye in Morristown, NJ, can be called Seeing Eye dogs.

ISBN 978-0-687-64478-0

08 09 10 11 12 13 14 15 16—10 9 8 7 6 5 4 3 2 1

Printed in China

Walter is a beautiful blond golden retriever who was born for a very special purpose. He works as a Seeing Eye® dog with Pastor Diane. Pastor Diane has difficulty seeing, and Walter's job is to guide her through the day so she can do her work of caring for the church.

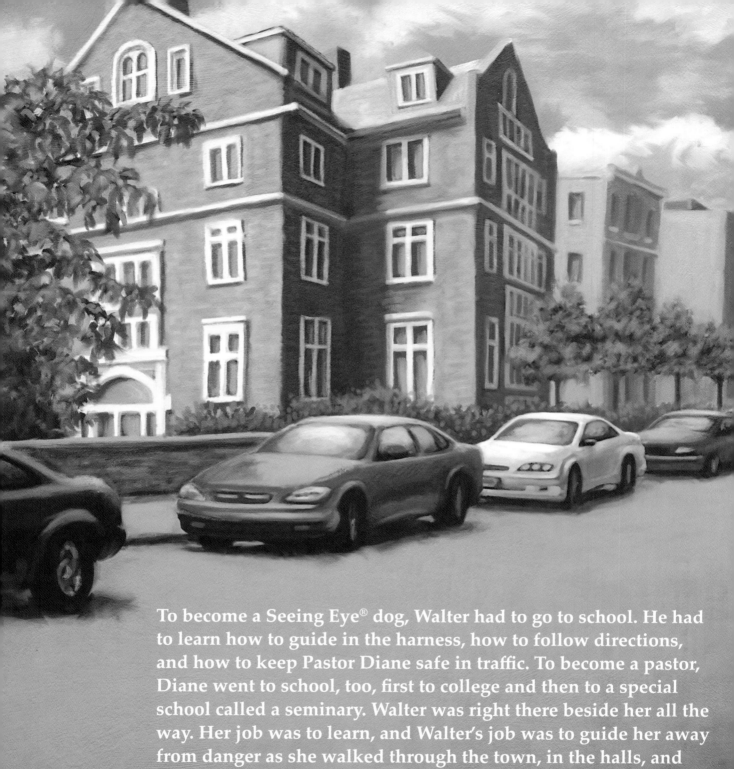

To become a Seeing Eye® dog, Walter had to go to school. He had to learn how to guide in the harness, how to follow directions, and how to keep Pastor Diane safe in traffic. To become a pastor, Diane went to school, too, first to college and then to a special school called a seminary. Walter was right there beside her all the way. Her job was to learn, and Walter's job was to guide her away from danger as she walked through the town, in the halls, and around the school grounds. They worked very well together.

When Diane graduated, she was ready to become a pastor. Together Walter and Diane went to a ceremony called an ordination. The bishop prayed a blessing prayer. Some of the people wore long robes over their clothes. These robes helped the congregation know which people were the pastors. Over the robes most wore long red scarves called stoles. After the ordination, it was decided that Walter and the new pastor would go to a church downtown to begin their ministry together. They were very happy.

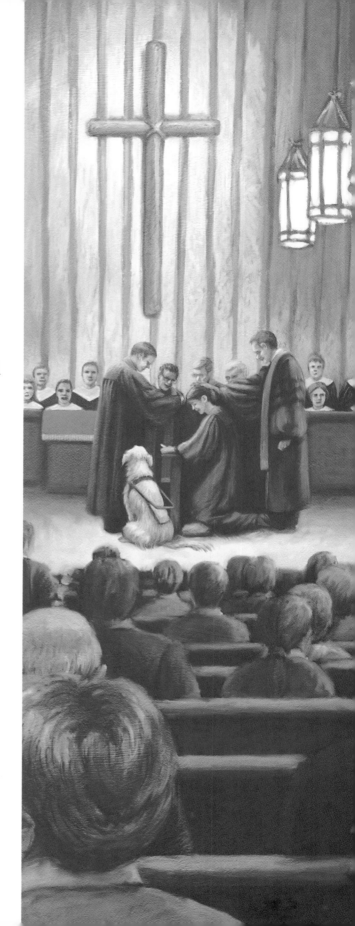

Now, Walter guides Pastor Diane down the sidewalk each day to the big church downtown and sits in Pastor Diane's study as she works. As Walter lies on his big green pillow under the desk, he can see many different people come to visit with Pastor Diane. Some people come to plan Sunday services. Other people come to talk about their worries, to pray, or to find help with their lives. Pastor Diane tries hard to help everyone who comes to see her.

On Monday, Pastor Diane begins to write the church newsletter. She types into her computer. Pastor Diane and Walter hear the computer talking as she types. The talking of the computer helps Pastor Diane know what the screen says. Soon the newsletter is done, and they can go home for the day.

On Tuesday, Walter and Pastor Diane take a taxi to the hospital to visit sick people. Pastor Diane and Walter stop by the chaplain's office to find out what rooms they are to visit today. The chaplain is like a pastor, but one who works at a hospital instead of a church. The chaplain pats Walter's head, and Pastor Diane reminds the chaplain not to pet Walter while he is working. If Walter gets too many pats, he might forget to be careful, and Pastor Diane and Walter could get hurt. A hospital volunteer tells Pastor Diane how many doorways to count to find the rooms of the people she will visit. The patients are happy to see Pastor Diane. Before leaving, Pastor Diane holds each patient's hand and prays as Walter waits patiently.

Wednesday is a meeting day. Many people come to the meeting as Walter crawls under the table to nap. The meeting is about how the church will help neighborhood children collect new shoes and supplies for school children who need them. Some children do not have what they need, and school will soon start. On the wall is a picture of Jesus holding little children. The picture reminds Pastor Diane and the people at the church meeting that Jesus himself helped people. There are difficult problems to solve, but the church and Pastor Diane are determined to help people.

After the meeting, Walter and Pastor Diane walk down the street
to a restaurant for lunch. The hostess smiles as they come in the
door. They come here every day, and Walter likes to sit at the
second table. He hopes it is ready! Walter waits under the table
during lunch and takes a little nap.

Tonight is a potluck supper. Families come to the church at suppertime and bring a casserole or a dessert to share with others. They put their dishes on a long table and get ready to eat dinner together. The smell of good food makes Walter hungry. Pastor Diane brings a special meal for Walter. He is glad she has remembered him.

On Thursday morning, some folks come to the church to learn more about the Bible. Pastor Diane helps them read the verses and understand what each one has to say. Walter curls up nearby and listens as the people read together. Slowly, Walter falls asleep at the soothing sounds of their voices.

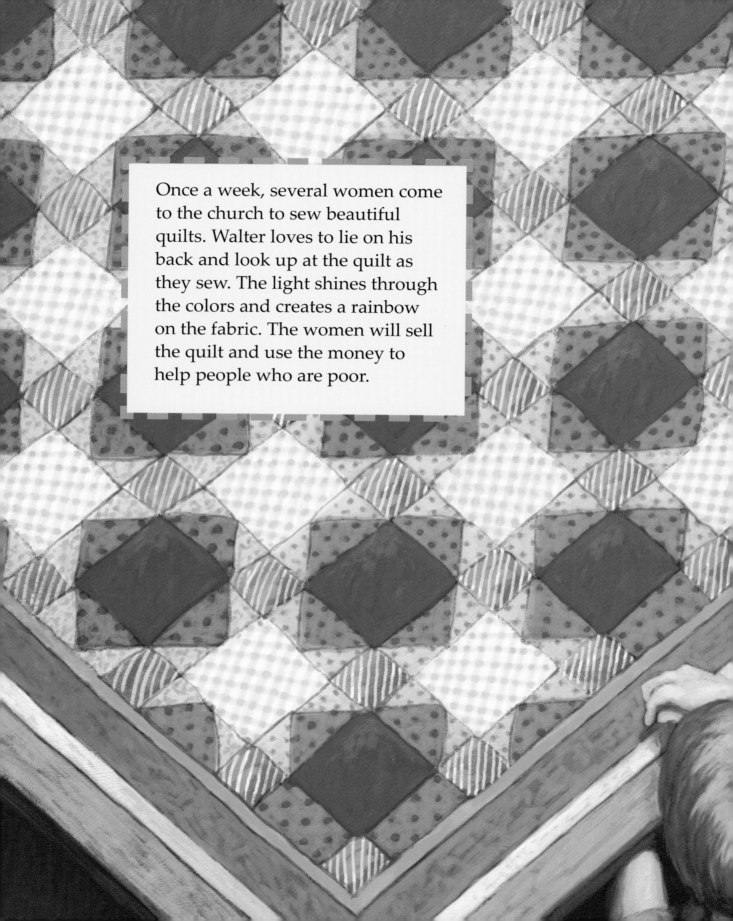

Once a week, several women come to the church to sew beautiful quilts. Walter loves to lie on his back and look up at the quilt as they sew. The light shines through the colors and creates a rainbow on the fabric. The women will sell the quilt and use the money to help people who are poor.

On Thursday afternoon, the chancel choir gathers in the sanctuary. They practice singing the music for Sunday's worship service. The choir director pauses to greet Walter. Walter wags his tail at her and crawls under a pew. Walter likes to listen to the choir sing. They sound like angels' voices. From under the pew, Walter sees the beautiful colors of the windows. As the sun shines through the stained-glass windows, the room glows.

On Friday, Walter and Pastor Diane arrive at the church and go into the main office. Many people work in the church office to prepare programs, called bulletins, to hand out on Sunday morning. Today they are having lunch together to talk about all the things the church will do in the coming months. They sit together in the church kitchen and pray before they eat their lunch. Walter eats his lunch, too, and then lies under the table for a nap. But, the sound of laughter makes Walter wake up. Pastor Diane gives him permission to say "Hello" to his friends. Walter nuzzles their hands one by one before settling back down at Pastor Diane's side.

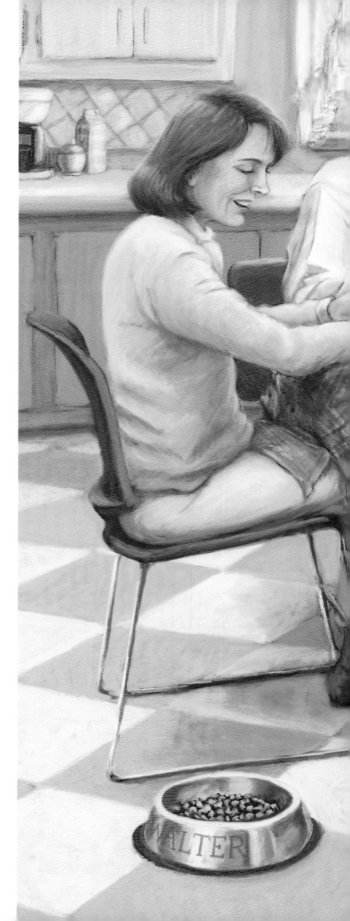

Finally, Sunday has come. It is the most important day of the week for Pastor Diane and Walter. They arrive at the church early in the morning. The choir director is getting the choir ready. The organist plays the big pipe organ. Ushers help the worshipers find a seat. They give each person a bulletin and a welcoming smile. Worship is ready to begin.

Walter guides Pastor Diane down the center aisle. They pause
together in front of the altar to pray. Walter guides Pastor
Diane up three steps toward a pew behind a tall, wooden box
called the pulpit. When Pastor Diane stands in the pulpit,
people can see her better and everyone can hear her preach.
Walter takes his place under the pew.

The view from under the pew is a wonderful view indeed. From under the pew Walter can look out and see the faces of families who have come to church to worship together. He can see the faces of older people who have come to this church since they were tiny babies. He can see the faces of people who have come here for the very first time today. The church is a very special place. And Walter is proud to work in ministry with Pastor Diane at the church.